# GOURMET CUPCAKES: FROM SCRATCH

# SIMPLE AND EASY

# BY

# ROSANNE ZINNIGER

**- second edition -**

ISBN—13: 978-1481217781

ISBN-10: 148121778X

First edition: December 9, 2012

Second edition: December 16, 2012

Printed in the United States of America

This Gourmet Cupcake book is a compilation of recipes that I have created and experimented with over the past few years, and have incorporated in my baking classes. Students have enjoyed them so much, they have asked me to write a book of recipes they can share with their friends and family! This is a second-edition with added ideas and a few minor corrections (lost in the first editing process). More books are to come, especially a recipe book all about cakes made from scratch!

Enjoy!

I am always excited to share! If you are interested in taking a class with me,

please pop on my website at

www.rozsweetartstudio.com

# TABLE OF CONTENTS

Base Recipe.................................... 9

Mojito Rosito ............................ 11

Peppermint Icing ............................ 12

Irish Mint Chocolate Chip ................... 13

Hazelnut Chocolate Frosting ................... 14

Chocolate Caramel Hazelnut ................... 15

Caramel Apple ..................................... 17

Brownie Cream Cheese ........................... 19

Pineapple Buttercream Frosting ................ 20

Tropical Coconut ...........................…....... 21

Spumoni Cake/Cupcakes........................... 22

Chocolate/Vanilla Marble........................ 25

Double Chocolate Mayonnaise ................ 27

Amazing Chocolate Frosting ................... 27

Kickin' Chocolate Chip ........................... 29

Slammin' Chocolate Stout ....................... 31

Vanilla Bean Sour Cream ....................... 33

Luscious Lemon ..................................... 35

Strawberry Cream ................................. 37

Resources ............................................. 38

Legend: C=cup; T=tablespoon, t=teaspoon

**Cupcakes** have overtaken the baking community and are so very popular at any event you can think of. Anyone can bake cupcakes by using a cake mix and following the directions; however, using simple and quality ingredients, you are sure to create a more flavorful and memorable cupcake. Make it Gourmet, by filling the center with a complimentary compote or a creamy mousse-like pudding, and decorate it with a flavorful frosting! I am happy to share the recipes I use along with tips and tricks to make your baking experience more efficient. Here are some tips to consider before baking:

- Begin with quality ingredients! Brand names are always better than store brands, as they are not "seconds" or ingredients have not been altered to distribute more of the product. Check the date on the package or container to purchase the freshest possible. This includes baking powder!

- Read the directions first, re-read, and follow the steps. All too often we are in a hurry and want to make it quick. Unfortunately, skipping a step or two will result in a poor quality end product.

- Sifting, and what it means in this book: if the recipe calls for sifting, be sure to read the directions. One cup flour, sifted means you should sift the flour after measuring. One cup sifted flour means you should sift before you measure. Spoon flour into your measuring cup instead of using the measuring cup to scoop the desired amount. If you have a kitchen scale, weigh your flour for accuracy.

- Cold eggs: in a hurry to bring to room temperature, put them in a bowl of warm water for 15 minutes. All of the cupcake recipes require room temperature eggs.

- Sugar: Pack brown sugar only—can use measuring cup to scoop the brown sugar to pack into the cup. For granulated and confectioner's sugar, spoon into the measuring cup as you would with flour. Or, better yet, use a kitchen scale to measure your sugar.

- Cold butter: to warm butter quicker, cut butter in small cubes and put them in a single layer on your pan. Set out for a half hour at room temperature for the butter to soften. Do not microwave butter to melt as you will change the chemistry of the butter consistency. I use unsalted butter in my recipes.

- Sour milk: if your recipe calls for sour milk, add 1 teaspoon of lemon juice or white vinegar to 1 cup of whole, low fat or non fat milk, and let stand for 10 minutes. I prefer lemon juice.

- Buttermilk: you can use dry buttermilk powder (which can be found in the baking aisle of most grocery stores) in your dry ingredients. Follow the directions on the powder buttermilk container. Usually I will add the buttermilk powder to the dry ingredients, and add the additional water required to my liquid ingredients. Although it is preferred to use the full fat liquid buttermilk in recipes, as the yields a better quality result.

- I use cake flour as it creates a more tender cupcake.

- Legend for this book: C = cup; T = tablespoon; t = teaspoon

Don't be afraid to try different add-in's and be creative! You never know what combination might be a winner with your friends and family!

Wishing you fun in the kitchen!

Ro Zinniger

**Base Cupcake Add-In's and Options:**

<u>For flavored cupcakes:</u>

Add LorAnn's Gourmet Flavor of your choice in place of Vanilla extract.

Add a whole vanilla bean: scrape the insides of a vanilla bean and add to batter during wet ingredient mixing.

Add Spices: add a teaspoon of cinnamon, ¼ teaspoon of ground cloves, and ¼ teaspoon of ground all-spice with a dash of ginger.

<u>For more flavor and texture:</u>

Add Chocolate chips or nuts or dried fruits—1/2 to 1 cup depending on your addition

# Base Cupcake Recipe

A base recipe is nice, as you can switch up flavors to match the season or holiday. Here is one I use:

**Ingredients:**

- 2 1/3 C Flour (I use Cake Flour)
- 1 T baking powder
- ½ t salt
- 1 ½ C granulated sugar
- ½ C oil
- 3 large eggs, room temperature
- 1 ½ C whole milk or coffee creamer (any flavor)
- 1 t Vanilla extract (or 1/2 t flavor of your choice)*
- 1/3 C sour cream

**Directions:**

Pre-heat oven to 350 degrees F. Line muffin pan with liners.

In a bowl, whisk flour, baking powder, and salt. In a mixing bowl, beat eggs, add sugar and beat until fluffy, then add oil, sour cream, and extract or flavor. Beat 2 minutes. While mixer is on low, add milk and flour mixture alternately, making sure all is combined, then beat for 1 minute on medium. Do not over mix or you will toughen your end product.

Pour batter in liners ½ to 2/3 full, do not over fill. Bake for 18 – 20 minutes. Check to see if they are done by lightly pressing on top of cupcake, if cake springs back then they are done. Remove from oven and place on a cooling rack. Frost when completely cooled. Yields: 36 cupcakes

* Flavor: LorAnn Gourmet Flavors are extremely potent and flavorful, along with their baking emulsions.

**Creating the Mojito Rosito:**

To enhance the flavors even more, insert mango filling in the center of the cupcake, top with a circle of melon-flavored rolled fondant and a green candy straw!

You will truly experience a party in your mouth with this combination!

# Mojito Rosito Cupcakes

This cupcake brings an explosion of flavors in your mouth in one small cake! I named it Mojito Rosito because it is a party in your mouth that I created! Pair it with a fresh squeezed lime Mojito Cocktail and you will want others to join your party too! (The recipe below is a lower calorie version, as it uses ½ the amount of sugar and milk instead of heavy whipping cream):

## Mojito Batter Ingredients:

½ C granulated sugar
1 ½ C Cake flour
¼ t salt
2 t baking powder
2 tsp LorAnn's Gourmet Key Lime Flavor
1 shot of Captain Morgan Spiced Rum
1 T of fresh mint, finely chopped
¼ C unsalted butter, room temperature
1 beaten large egg, room temperature
1 C whole milk

Preheat oven to 350 degrees F. Mix flour, salt, and baking powder together and set aside. Beat melted butter in a bowl, add sugar and cream, then add beaten egg to mixture. Add dry ingredients, combine, then slowly add milk, while stirring. Finally stir in rum and lime oil, then fold in mint.

Line a muffin or cupcake pan with liners and spoon batter in ½ to 2/3 full. Bake for 10 to 12 minutes. Cupcakes will be done when it is spongy to touch. Remove and cool on a rack. Top with a non-dairy whipped topping and a sprig of mint. Makes 12 to 18 cupcakes.

## Peppermint Icing
4 T butter, softened
2 C confectioners' sugar
2 t milk or cream
1 t peppermint LorAnn's Gourmet flavor

Mix all ingredients in a small bowl until smooth. Spread a medium thin layer on top of each cooled cupcake. Or, use a #1M decorator tip with icing in a decorator bag and swirl the icing on your cupcake.

Top with crushed peppermint candies!

# Irish Mint Chocolate Chip Cupcakes

You can make this recipe anytime, although these are festive for the holiday season!

**Ingredients:**
1 1/3 C cake flour
1/2 t baking powder
1/4 t baking soda
1/4 t salt
1/3 C unsalted butter, room temperature
1 C granulated sugar
2 large eggs, room temperature
1 t vanilla extract
1/2 C Bailey's Irish Cream
1/2 t peppermint LorAnn's Gourmet flavor (or 1 t peppermint extract)
1/4 C whole milk
2/3 C mini chocolate chips

Preheat oven to 350F. Line baking tin of your choice – mini muffin pan or regular cupcake pan – with paper liners.

In a small bowl, whisk together flour, baking powder, baking soda and salt. In a large bowl, cream together butter and sugar until light and fluffy. Beat in eggs one at a time, followed by vanilla extract and peppermint flavor. Mix in half of the flour mixture, followed by the Bailey's Irish Cream and milk, then mix in the remaining flour mixture, ending with the cream/milk. Stir in chocolate chips.

Distribute batter evenly into prepared liners (each will be roughly 2/3 or 3/4 full) Bake regular-sized cupcakes for 22-25 minutes.  Bake mini cupcakes for 10-12 minutes.
Tops should be domed, springy to touch, and very lightly browned. Cool on a wire rack 15 minutes before frosting.
Yields 24 cupcakes.

## <u>Hazelnut Chocolate Frosting:</u>

- 3 C powdered sugar
- 1/4 C Nutella
- 6 T unsalted butter, room temperature
- Hazelnut Creamer—add to desired
- Consistency
- Chocolate shavings

Mix the above until you achieve a creamy consistency.

"Swirl" icing on cupcakes with a #1M tip, then drizzle caramel sauce and top with chocolate shavings!

# Chocolate Caramel Hazelnut Cupcakes

**Ingredients:**
   2 C granulated sugar
   1 C all-purpose flour (King Arthur is preferred)
   ¾ C freshly ground hazelnuts
   ¾ C cocoa powder (Callebaut brand)
   1 1/2 t baking powder
   1 1/2 t baking soda
   1 t salt
   3/4 t LorAnn's Chocolate Hazelnut Flavor
   ¾ C sour cream
   2 large eggs, room temperature
   1/2 C Pacifica Culinaria Avocado oil
   1 C whole milk
   Caramel bits, add 2-3 per cupcake liner
   Nutella, ¾ C (optional)

**Instructions:**
Preheat oven to 350 degrees F.

Sift together the sugar, flour, freshly ground hazelnuts, cocoa powder, baking powder, baking soda, and salt; set aside. In a separate bowl, briefly whisk together the sour cream and vanilla extract; set aside. In the bowl of a mixer fitted with a paddle attachment (Beater Blade preferred), beat together the eggs, vegetable oil, and milk, until smooth. Add the sour cream mixture and stir until well incorporated. You may choose to add Nutella at this point in the mixing process—optional. Add the flour mixture until incorporated, do not overbeat. Batter should be thin. Fill each liner with 2 or 3 caramel bits, then fill with batter ½ to 2/3 full. Bake for 20 minutes or when cake springs back. Cool on cooling rack for 15 minutes. Makes 24 cupcakes.

## Finishing Touches:

After cupcake is cooled, fill the center with an apple compote or apple filling with caramel sauce

Frost with an apple flavored buttercream or create a cupcake cap with Fondant – red, add a green fondant leaf to the top for a finishing touch!

### Apple Compote

- 3lb apples, peeled, cored and cut into 1 inch chunks
- 2 T fresh lemon juice
- 1 T apple brandy
- ¼ C granulated sugar
- ¼ t ground all spice
- ¼ t ground cinnamon
- 1/4 C raisins—optional

Combine all ingredients in a large pot, cover and cook over low heat, stirring occasionally – until apples are tender. About 30 minutes. Let compote cool completely.

# Gourmet Caramel Apple Cupcakes

**Ingredients:**

 2  1/3 C Cake Flour
 1 T baking powder
 ½ t salt
 1 t ground cinnamon
 ¼ t nutmeg or allspice
 1 ½ C white granulated sugar
 1/3 C oil (can use Pacifica Culinaria Avocado Oil)
 3 large eggs, room temperature
 1 ½ C milk or coffee creamer (Caramel flavor is nice)
 1 t LorAnn's Gourmet Apple Flavor
 1/3 C sour cream
 ½ C caramel bits

**Directions:**

Pre-heat oven to 350 degrees F. Line muffin pan with liners. In a bowl, whisk flour, baking powder, spices and salt.  In a mixing bowl, beat eggs, add sugar and beat until fluffy, then add oil, sour cream, and apple flavor. Beat 2 minutes. While mixer is on low, add milk and flour mixture alternately, making sure all is combined, then beat for 1 minute on medium. Do not over mix or you will toughen your end product.

Pour batter in liners ½ to 2/3 full, do not over pour. Add the caramel bits to the center of the batter. Bake for 18 – 20 minutes. Check to see if they are done by lightly pressing on top of cupcake, if cake springs back then they are done.

Remove from oven and place on a cooling rack. Fill and Frost when completely cooled. Makes 36 cupcakes.

**Finishing touches:**

**If you want to make this Gour-
met cupcake more decadent,
add cherry filling in the center
and top with whipped cream,
nuts and a cherry on top!
OR
Cover with Satin Ice Pink Fondant and create leaves and a
rose for decoration! A pretty
cupcake wrap makes it a
"Couture Gourmet Cupcake".**

# Brownie Cream Cheese Gourmet Cupcakes

I created these yummy cupcakes for the 2010 Celebrity Chefs Tour. The audience was not disappointed, and I am sure you won't be either!

Pre-heat oven to 350 degrees F
Bake 20-25 minutes
Yield: 24 Flavorful Cupcakes

**Batter Ingredients:**
>    1 ¼ C cake flour
>    1 C granulated sugar
>    ¼ C unsweetened cocoa powder (Callebaut Brand)
>    1 t baking soda
>    Pinch of salt

Sift all above together in a bowl
>    1 large egg, room temperature
>    ¼ C vegetable oil
>    ¼ C sour cream
>    1 t Madagascar vanilla extract or 1/2 t vanilla LorAnn's oil
>    1 t apple cider vinegar

Cream all wet ingredients in a small bowl

At low speed, beat wet ingredients into dry ingredients until a smooth batter forms. The batter will be stiff not creamy.

**Filling ingredients:**
>    8 oz. cream cheese, at room temperature
>    1/3 C granulated sugar
>    1 large egg, room temperature
>    1/8 t salt

Cream the above, then add 1 C mini chocolate chips
Use standard or jumbo cupcake pan with jumbo cupcake liners. Spoon batter, then a heaping teaspoon of filling into the center of each batter cavity. Bake. Cool 10 minutes. Enjoy warm with vanilla ice cream and a sprig of mint!

## **Pineapple Buttercream Frosting:**

4 C powdered sugar
1 t meringue powder
Pinch of salt
½ C unsalted butter, room temperature
½ C hi-ratio shortening (or vegetable shortening)
2 t Amoretti Pineapple Compound or Pineapple extract
3 T Water
Cream all ingredients until smooth. Make sure consistency is soft and thin. If too stiff add another tablespoon of water. Store in refrigerator until ready to use. Bring to room temperature to pipe with.

# Tropical Coconut Gourmet Cupcakes

This is another recipe I created for the Celebrity Chefs Tour.

Makes 36
Pre-heat oven 350 degrees F
    Bake 20-25 min.

**Ingredients:**
- 2 ¼ C cake flour
- 2 t baking powder
- ½ t salt
- ½ C sweetened flake coconut (optional)
- 1 ½ C unsalted butter, room temperature
- 1 C granulated sugar
- 1 T coconut baking emulsion by LorAnn's Gourmet
- 3 large eggs, room temperature
- 3/4 C coconut milk

Pre-heat oven and line cupcake pan with baking liners. In a bowl, whisk flour, baking powder, salt and coconut. In a mixing bowl, cream butter and sugar, add the emulsion, and beat for 3 minutes. Add eggs one at a time. Add in dry ingredients alternating with coconut milk until smooth.
Spoon in lined pan cavities ½- 2/3 full. Bake. Cool 10 minutes. Frost.

Idea: Fill cupcake with Pineapple filling and sweetened coconut flake, then decorate with pineapple buttercream frosting. To create a tropical version, add 1/2 t of LorAnn's Gourmet Piña Colada flavor in the batter in addition to the emulsion. Top with shredded coconut and serve with a tropical drink!

# Ro Z's Spumoni Cake or Cupcakes

You will be creating a base recipe then will separate to create cherry, pistachio and chocolate batter. It may be a little time consuming, however the result is quite fabulous! Your friends and family will agree!

**Base Batter Ingredients:**

- ½ C unsalted butter, room temperature
- 1 ¾ C cake flour
- 2 t baking powder
- ½ t salt
- ¾ C granulated sugar
- 2 large eggs, room temperature
- 1 t almond extract
- ½ C milk, whole is preferred

Preheat oven to 375 degrees F. In a mixing bowl, whisk all dry ingredients well = flour, salt, baking powder, set aside. In a mixing bowl with paddle attachment, beat butter, slowly add sugar, and beat mixture until aerated (2 minutes).

Beat in one egg at a time until well beaten, add extract and mix well. On lowest speed, add in alternately the flour mixture and milk a third at a time. Mix until well incorporated and batter is smooth. Do not over mix. Batter yields 3 cups.

Follow instructions on next page.

In 3 separate bowls, add one cup each of the batter. Then follow the directions below:

Batter bowl 1 = Chocolate: Melt 2 oz. dark chocolate. When cool, fold chocolate into batter.

Batter bowl 2 = Cherry: Fold in ¼ t LorAnn Cherry flavor oil and ½ C candied cherries – quartered (or Marschino Cherries).

Batter bowl 3 = Pistachio: Fold in ¼ t LorAnn Pistachio flavor oil and 1 heaping T pistachio paste*

For cupcakes: fill disposable bags (3) each with batter. One squeeze (1 T) batter each/per liner, should be ½ to 2/3 full. Bake 15-18 minutes. Yields 24 cupcakes. Top with a Cannoli filling (can be found at specialty markets) and chopped pistachios.

For cake: layer the batter mixtures. Bake 35-45 in (2) 9" pans.

## *Pistachio Paste Recipe
Yield 1 – ½ Cup

1 C unsalted pistachios, shells and skins removed (if salted, wash well)
¼ C granulated sugar
½ C hot water
2 oz. Pistachio instant pudding mix (or vanilla flavor)
In a food processor, grind pistachios until almost fine. Add sugar and pudding mix, and mix until well combined. Add water slowly and mix until a spreadable paste forms. Note: you may not have to add all of the water. Transfer to glass bowl and refrigerate.

Create Gourmet Couture Cupcakes by decorating with a simple flavored buttercream frosting (any flavor you desire) and create a center swirl then drizzle with chocolate sauce!

Idea: Fill cupcake with chocolate sauce and top with vanilla buttercream (use Pineapple buttercream recipe and substitute 1/2 vanilla bean and 2 t vanilla extract.

# Chocolate / Vanilla Marble Cupcakes

These simple cupcakes are a favorite with all ages!

## Ingredients:

    1 ¾ C cake flour sifted
    2 t baking powder
    ½ t salt
    ½ C whole milk, room temperature
    1/3 C heavy cream, room temperature
    ½ C unsalted butter, room temperature
    1 C granulated sugar
    3 large eggs, room temperature
    1 T LorAnn's Gourmet Vanilla Bean paste
    1/3 C unsweetened cocoa powder (Callebaut brand)
    ¼ C boiling water

## PREPARATION

Preheat oven to 350 degrees F. Line standard cupcake tins with paper liners. Sift together cake flour, baking powder, and salt in a bowl and set aside. Combine milk and cream in another bowl and set aside. In a mixing bowl, cream butter and granulated sugar until pale and fluffy – about 3 minutes. Add eggs. One at a time, beating until each is incorporated. Beat in vanilla. Add flour mixture in three batches, alternating with two additions of milk mixture, and beating until combined. To make chocolate batter, measure out 1 cup batter, and transfer to another bowl and set aside. Combine cocoa and the boiling water in a bowl. Stir into reserved 1 cup batter.

Fill prepared liners with alternating spoonfuls of vanilla and chocolate batter, filling each liner 1/2 full. You may choose to swirl batter with the tip of a knife. Bake 18 to 20 minutes until cupcakes are springy to the touch. Remove from oven, and cool. Cupcakes can be stored overnight at room temperature or frozen up to 1 month in airtight containers. Makes 24.

**Amazing Chocolate Frosting Steps:**
Use frosting ingredients from next page: Place chopped chocolate in medium metal bowl; set bowl over saucepan of simmering water and stir until chocolate is melted and smooth. Carefully remove bowl from over water; let melted chocolate cool until lukewarm, stirring occasionally. Using electric mixer, beat butter in large bowl until smooth and creamy. Sift powdered sugar over butter and beat until well blended, about 2 minutes. Beat in vanilla. Add melted chocolate and beat until well blended and smooth, occasionally scraping down sides of bowl. Ready to pipe on your cooled cupcakes!

Idea: Fill with chocolate sauce and frost with Amazing Chocolate Frosting recipe! Serve with a side of vanilla ice cream!

# Double Chocolate Mayonnaise Cupcakes

## Batter Ingredients
2 oz bittersweet chocolate (do not exceed 61% cacao), chopped
2/3 C unsweetened cocoa powder
1 3/4 C boiling water
2 3/4 C cake flour
1 1/4 t baking soda
1/4 t baking powder
1 C granulated sugar
1 C (packed) dark brown sugar
1 1/3 C mayonnaise (full fat)
2 large eggs, room temperature
1 t Madagascar vanilla extract
1/2 C dark chocolate chips

## Amazing Chocolate Frosting:
10 oz bittersweet chocolate (do not exceed 61% cacao), chopped
1 1/2 cups unsalted butter, room temperature
3 C powdered sugar
1 T vanilla extract

Preheat oven to 350°F. Prepare cupcake pans and add liners. Combine chopped chocolate and cocoa powder in medium metal bowl. Add 1 3/4 cups boiling water and whisk until chocolate is melted and mixture is smooth.

In another bowl, sift flour, baking soda, and baking powder. Using electric mixer, beat sugars and mayonnaise in large bowl until well blended, 2 to 3 minutes. Add eggs 1 at a time, beating until well blended after each addition. Beat in vanilla. Add flour mixture in 4 additions alternately with chocolate mixture in 3 additions (end with wet ingredients), beating until blended after each addition. Add chocolate chips. Divide batter evenly among lined cupcake cavities. Bake cupcakes 20-22 minutes. Makes 36.

## Kickin' Chocolate Chip Finishing!

Make the Amazing Chocolate Frosting recipe from page 26, and add 1/2 t LorAnn's Gourmet Hot Chili Flavor, and mix until the frosting has a creamy consistency. Swirl frosting on cupcake, top with crushed cinnamon candies!

<u>Make it unique:</u>

A vanilla buttercream tinted green (or any color) in a decorator bag with a frill tip makes nice ruffles. Top with a fondant daisy accented with a fondant ribbon rose.

# Kickin' Chocolate Chip Cupcakes

## Batter Ingredients:

1/2 C unsalted butter, room temperature
6 T granulated sugar
6 T brown sugar, packed
1 large egg, room temperature
1 C plus 2 T Cake Flour
½ t baking soda
½ t salt
2 t Madagascar Vanilla extract

## Filling Ingredients:

½ C brown sugar
1 large egg, room temperature
1/8 t salt
1 C chocolate chips, dark preferred
½ C nuts – optional

Preheat oven to 350 degrees F. In a large bowl, cream the butter and sugars until light and fluffy. Beat in egg and vanilla. In another bowl, whisk flour, baking soda, salt, then gradually add dry ingredients to wet ingredients. Line cupcake pans with liners, and fill liner ½ full of batter. Bake for 10 minutes or until top appears set. For Filling: Beat brown sugar, egg and salt until combined, then stir in chocolate chips and nuts. Once the batter is baked to set, add a tablespoon to the center of each cupcake. Bake an additional 10 minutes. Remove from oven to cooling rack for 15 minutes.

**Simple Vanilla Buttercream Swirl topped with Sixlet candies on top works nicely!**

# SLAMMIN' CHOCOLATE STOUT CUPCAKES

After a little experimentation, I found the chocolate flavor is enhanced with a darker beer / Ale!

## Ingredients:

1 ½ C Cake Flour
1 C granulated sugar
1 tsp baking soda
¼ C unsweetened dark Cocoa powder (Callebaut brand)
1/3 C oil (light extra virgin olive oil is great)
1 T cider vinegar
1 t vanilla bean emulsion
1 C Chocolate Stout Ale (or Dark Guiness)

## Filling:

8 oz Mascarpone cheese
1 large egg at room temperature
1/3 C granulated sugar
1/8 t salt
6 oz. chocolate chips
½ C finely chopped pecans – optional

Preheat oven to 350 degrees F. Prepare cupcake pans with liners. Combine flour, sugar, baking soda, cocoa and salt in a bowl. In another mixing bowl, add oil, vinegar, beer and vanilla beating well. Add the dry combination slowly. Make Filling: Combine cheese, egg, sugar, salt, chocolate chips and nuts. Fill liners 1/3 full with batter, then top each with a heaping tsp of cheese mixture.  Bake 18—20 minutes. Please note that the middle will be liquid until it cools – approximately 15 minutes. Idea: serve with a chocolate stout float (vanilla ice cream in a chocolate stout ale!

Tip: It is nice to work with a mixer with horsepower and a Beater Blade (which scrapes the bowl as the blade turns). Great equipment makes for a more efficient process!

# VANILLA BEAN SOUR CREAM CUPCAKES

Yield: Makes 48 Cupcakes
Pre-heat Oven: 350 degrees F
Baking time: 12-15 minutes

## Ingredients:

3 1/2 C cake flour
1 T baking powder
3/4 t baking soda
1 t salt
1 C unsalted butter, softened
2 C sugar
4 large eggs, room temperature
1 T LorAnn's Gourmet vanilla bean paste
2 t Madagascar vanilla extract
2 C sour cream

## The Steps:

Preheat oven to 350°F. Prepare cupcake pans with liners.

In separate bowl, sift together flour, baking powder, baking soda, and salt. Beat together butter and sugar in a large bowl with an electric mixer until light and fluffy – about 3 full minutes. Add eggs 1 at a time, beating well after each addition, then beat in vanilla bean and vanilla extract. Alternate adding flour mixture and sour cream: Add half of flour mixture and mix at low speed until just blended. Add sour cream, mixing until just combined, then add remaining flour mixture, mixing at low speed until batter is smooth.

Fill liners ½ full. Bake between 12-15 minutes. Bake in middle of oven until cake is springy to the touch and a tester comes out clean. Cool in pans on cooling rack for 15 minutes. Then remove from pan and decorate as desirable.

Since this recipe is so lemony, you might want to put a glaze on the cupcakes and a sprig of mint! Great for those lemon lovers in your life!

# Luscious Lemon Cupcakes

It is always nice to have some base flavorful recipes to go to. There are many recipes out there, however this recipe is the one I endorse, and you will find you will too!

## Batter Ingredients:

- ¾ C unsalted butter, room temperature
- 2 C cake flour
- 4 washed lemons, cut ends – discard, slice thinly
- ½ t salt
- 2 C granulated sugar (can substitute 1 C Agave syrup*)
- 2 large eggs plus 2 egg yolks, room temperature (save egg whites)
- 1 t baking powder
- 2/3 C whole milk (reduce milk to 1/3 C if you add Agave syrup*)
- 2 t Madagascar vanilla extract

Preheat oven: 375 degrees F, and prepare cupcake pan with liners. In a bowl, whisk flour, salt, baking powder, set aside.

Lemon mixture: In a medium saucepan, add lemon slices, 3 cups of water, a pinch of salt, and cover. Bring to a boil at high heat, and boil until lemons are very tender – approximately 15 minutes. Drain and transfer to a food processor. Add butter and process until smooth.

Transfer lemon mixture to a mixing bowl, and beat in sugar, eggs – one at a time and egg yolks and vanilla extract until combined. With mixer on slow, add flour mixture and milk alternately in a 1/3 at a time. Mix until batter is smooth, however do not over mix. Fill liners ½ full with batter. Bake until golden brown approximately 14-18 minutes. Let cool on cooling rack 20 minutes. Frost with a lemon buttercream icing.
* Organic Agave syrup used is by Pacifica Culinaria. Do not use Blue Agave, as the taste can be too strong.

**Prepare the filling:** Combine the cream cheese (or mascarpone) and sugar and beat for 1 minute. Beat in the cream, sugar and vanilla; beat until creamy and smooth, scraping side of bowl.

**Prepare the topping:** Beat 1 1/2 cups cream until stiff peaks begin to form. Beat in sugar and vanilla.

# STRAWBERRY CREAM CUPCAKES

## Batter Ingredients:
1 1/4 C cake flour
1/2 t baking soda
1/4 t fine sea salt
3/4 C granulated sugar (divided use (1/2 for batter / ½ for egg whites)
1/2 C whole buttermilk
1/4 C applesauce
1/2 t  LorAnn's Gourmet Strawberry Flavor (or 1 t vanilla extract)
3 large eggs, separated – room temperature
1 t lemon zest
1 T fresh lemon juice
1 C strawberries, puree lightly

## Cheese Mixture to insert:
3 oz cream cheese or Mascarpone cheese
1 T granulated sugar*
1/2 C heavy cream
1/2 t vanilla extract

## Topping:
1 1/2 C whipping cream
2 1/2 T granulated sugar**
1 1/2 t vanilla extract

Preheat oven to 350 degrees F (180 degrees C). Combine the flour, baking soda, salt and 1/2 cup of the granulated sugar in a mixing bowl and stir well. Whisk the buttermilk, apple sauce, vanilla and egg yolks together in a second bowl, then add to flour mixture and stir until smooth. Add lemon zest and lemon juice and mix well. Whip egg whites until soft peaks form. Slowly add the reserved ¼ cup sugar to the whites. Whisk the batter into the egg whites until well blended. Pour the batter into liners. Bake on center rack for 30-35 minutes or until a toothpick inserted in center comes out clean. Cool for 10-15 minutes.
* Sweeten to taste — 1 tablespoon was enough, but you may want more or less.
**Taste as you go. You might want to use up to 3 T sugar.

# RESOURCES

**Fat Daddio's**          (800) 418-9001

PO Box 30175, Spokane, WA 99223

www.fatdaddios.com / E-Mail: info@fatdaddios.com

(Professional bakeware and decorating supplies)


**Satin Fine Foods, Inc.**    (845) 469-1034

32 Leone Lane, Unit 1, Chester, NY 10918

www.satinice.com / E-Mail: contact @ satinfinefoods.com

(Fondant and Gumpaste Manufacturer)


**Pacifica Culinaria**        (800) 622-8880

PO Box 507, Vista, CA 92085

www.pacificaculinaria.com / E-Mail: csivista@aol.com

(Gourmet oils, Agave Syrup, Vinegars)

# RESOURCES

**Ro Z's Sweet Art Studio**        760-744-0447

277 S. Rancho Santa Fe Road, San Marcos, CA 92078

www.rozsweetartstudio.com / E-Mail: rozsweetart@att.net

(Classes/workshops; baking supplies; and private instruction)


**LorAnn Oil's, Inc.**        (800) 862-8620

4518 Aurelius Road, Lansing, MI 48910

www.lorannoils.com / customercare@lorannoils.com

(Gourmet flavors, oils and baking emulsions)


**New Metro Design, Inc.**        (800) 624-1526

www.newmetrodesign.com / E-Mail: info@newmetrodesign.com

(Beater Blade, JuiceLab, ZestN'est, MixerMate)

**Dear Readers,**

**I am so happy to share my gourmet cupcake and frosting recipes with you! I hope you enjoy them and share them with your family and friends!**

**Sweet Regards,**

*Rosanne Zinniger (a.k.a. Ro Zinniger),*

*Owner of Ro-Z's Sweet Art Studio in San Diego, CA*

**www.rozsweetartstudio.com**

Made in United States
North Haven, CT
19 December 2021

13283319R00024